Sharing our Journey

This is the second edition of a booklet published by Dumbarton United Methodist Church in 1988, shortly after we completed a process of inquiry and dialogue about whether to publicly welcome lesbian and gay people into the full life of our church.

In 1984, the delegate assembly of our denomination had declared that "homosexuality is incompatible with Christian teaching" and warned that no "self-avowed practicing homosexual" would be ordained or assigned to parish ministry and that no church funds would be spent to "promote the acceptance of homosexuality."

These statements mirrored those being passed by the governing bodies of other denominations, yet many faithful Christians disagreed. Groups had begun forming in each denomination to give voice to another perspective—that whatever our sexual orientation, each of us is a child of God, and God loves each one.

Initially, members wondered why we were even talking about welcoming gay and lesbian people, believing (incorrectly) that we didn't have any in our church. But we proceeded to talk about sexuality, read the Bible, argue, sing, preach, laugh, cry, and pray. Eventually, we voted and unanimously affirmed that as a Christian community, we indeed welcome everyone, specifically naming gay/lesbian people and their families. Recently, we expanded our welcome to bisexual and transgender people.

During this period, our congregation has thrived and grown. And what's more, we've raised an entire generation of children in this context of wider welcome—children who can stand up to name-calling and bullying at school and in their neighborhoods because they know gay people as friends and parents of friends, Sunday School teachers, and clergy.

We've published this booklet to share the richness of our own experience, bringing together for other people of faith the information and perspectives that have been important to us in our journey.

This booklet, then, is about sexual orientation—heterosexual, gay, lesbian, and bisexual. You may already know people who have a different sexual orientation than you do and you're reading this booklet to gain a better understanding.

Or you may be gay, lesbian, or bisexual—or the child, parent,

Expanding our welcome has enriched our life as a community.

or family member of someone who is—and eager to find an affirming, religiously oriented resource that addresses your concerns and questions.

Or you may be curious or even somewhat skeptical, feeling that in your particular religious community (or neighborhood or school or workplace), it's not really an issue, because "we don't have any gay people here."

Don't believe it. No matter where you live, children and adults are suffering because the clear message they hear from much of society, especially the religious community, is that they should change, that it's wrong to be who they are, that who they are is unacceptable and unforgivable.

There are also children, youth, and adults among you who love someone who is lesbian, gay, or bisexual—perhaps a parent or child, sibling, aunt, uncle, cousin, colleague, close friend, or clergy. As you read this booklet, consider that the religious condemnation of non-heterosexual orientation affects nearly everyone.

The people whose photos appear on pages 2–16 reflect the diversity among gay/lesbian/bisexual people. Some are Christian; others are not.

Many gay people have left the church; some left because they'd been sent away. Others have gone to worship with or serve other religious groups. Still others have left altogether, some sadly, many with great bitterness. We may not know why they left, but their leaving is a tremendous loss to all of us.

But many have stayed and are serving as clergy and laypersons—faithfully calling the church to a new dialogue.

Theirs is a powerful witness. Your openness to new possibilities is also a powerful witness. God be with you.

Sexuality

a good gift of God

Sexuality is a good gift of God, and we believe persons may be fully human only when that gift is acknowledged and affirmed by themselves, the Church, and society.

—*Book of Social Principles*
United Methodist Church

Let's face it. Americans bring sex into everything from toothpaste to cars, yet most of us have a hard time affirming sexuality as a "good gift of God."

And if it's hard to talk about sexuality in an open, honest, caring way, it may seem nearly impossible to talk about differences in sexual orientation. One reason is that when people think "sex," they tend to think of sexual *behavior.* But sexuality encompasses a lot more than behavior.

Sexuality is how we understand and express our gender; how we grow and change over the years; how we view our bodies; how we relate to each other; whom we like, love, and are attracted to; how we reproduce; how we're alike and different in appearance and behavior; what we believe is important; and much, much more.

Sexuality includes biological sex.

Given that every newborn is greeted with the same question—*Is it a boy or a girl?*—biological sex can appear to be the most fundamental aspect of our sexuality.

Yet even that simple question doesn't always have a simple answer. Some babies have physical characteristics that lead to confusion about whether they're male or female. For other babies, atypical aspects of physical, genetic, and brain sex may be invisible at birth and become apparent in early childhood, at puberty, or even later when genetic tests are performed.

In addition, our biological sex may not match our gender identity, which is how we see ourselves on the spectrum of female and male, what we let the world see about us, and how congruent our bodies are with our internal experience.

Biological sex and gender diversity are explained more fully in our companion book, *Made in God's Image.*

Photo © *San Francisco Chronicle,* Liz Mangelsdorf

Our sexuality begins at conception and unfolds throughout our lifetime.

Sexuality includes gender roles.

Real variations in physical sex notwithstanding, parents do label their child as a boy or a girl, and from that moment on, children begin learning what's considered appropriate for them as boys or girls and what's not.

One gender role expectation that children learn early is not to act "gay" or not to act like a "sissy," "faggot," or "dyke." Rather than be free to be themselves, boys and girls learn to stifle anything that might be considered "wrong"—too feminine for boys or too masculine for girls.

These playground rules, which extend into adult relationships, demonstrate that people confuse *gender role* with *sexual orientation*, which will be discussed shortly.

Sexuality includes sensuality and intimacy.

Sexuality includes being sensual, which has to do with the ways we feel pleasure, our comfort with touching and feelings, the image we have of our bodies, how we accept ourselves, what we know about our bodies, and how we take care of them.

Sexuality also includes intimacy, which has to do with our ability to trust another person, to become known, to share, to show affection, to reveal ourselves honestly, and to allow others to reveal themselves to us.

Sexuality includes behavior.

Sexual behavior includes how we walk and talk, how we dress, how we express affection. When people use the term "having sex," they're talking about a subset of a huge range of behaviors, from holding hands to kissing to various forms of giving and receiving pleasure, including different kinds of sexual intercourse.

Sexuality includes sexual orientation.

Sexual orientation refers to the sex of the people to whom we're physically and romantically attracted. We discover our own orientation by noticing our dreams, fantasies, longings, physical and emotional arousal, comfort, and love.

Sexual orientation is our internal experience of being physically and romantically attracted to someone.

Please note that when people say they're heterosexual, they're indicating only their internal *sexual orientation*, not their sexual *behavior*. For example, a woman who identifies herself as heterosexual is simply saying that she's attracted, physically and romantically, to men. She isn't saying that she's attracted to *all* men, nor is she saying that, at the moment, she acts on her attraction.

So it is with homosexuality (gay or lesbian) and bisexuality, which are also *sexual orientations*. Gay males find that the people they're attracted to, physically and romantically, are other males; lesbians find that the people they're attracted to are other women. Bisexual people find that they're attracted to some people who are male and some who are female.

Like heterosexuality, the terms *homosexuality* and *bisexuality* describe an internal experience that's unique for each person.

And sexuality includes identity.

Our identity is who we say we are to ourselves and to others. But a person's identity, orientation, and behavior don't always line up. For example, a bisexual woman may be married to a man. Her internal orientation is bisexual, but unless she specifically talks about it, people will probably assume that she's heterosexual.

Or a man who's uncomfortable with his attraction to other men may insist, both to himself and to others, that he's heterosexual. Unless he specifically talks about his attraction to men, people will assume that he's heterosexual.

Photo © Limor Inbar/Indelible Images

Or a woman who understands herself to be lesbian and has a long-time woman partner may feel that her workplace isn't a safe place to be "out," so she allows others to assume that she's a single, heterosexual woman and tries to deal graciously with their efforts to help her find a man.

So you can see that people's sexual identity—both their private understanding of their sexual orientation and the public image they project—may not align with their relationships and behavior.

You may have wondered...

Photo © Joan E. Biren/QueerStock

What causes a person's sexual orientation?

We don't know what causes heterosexuality, much less what causes homosexuality or bisexuality. Just as heterosexual people come from all walks of life and all types of family, religious, and cultural backgrounds, so do lesbian, gay, and bisexual people.

Why do people choose to be gay, lesbian, or bisexual?

First, think about the heterosexual people you know. They probably don't have a sense of having chosen to be that way; it just came naturally. That's the way it is for gay, lesbian, and bisexual people as well. Looking back, many say that they came to recognize their sexual orientation fairly early in childhood.

A person's orientation isn't chosen, but rather discovered. Discovering your sexual orientation is a little like putting together the pieces to a puzzle—sensual feelings, fantasies, dreams, attractions, crushes, and so on.

So the choice for all of us is not *whether* to be heterosexual, gay, lesbian, or bisexual, but *how* to be whoever we are. The question is whether we'll choose to behave in ways that are caring or exploitative, selfish or nurturing, violent or loving.

Why don't gay, lesbian, and bisexual people change?

This question implies that something needs to be fixed—but there's really nothing wrong. Homosexuality and bisexuality are normal variations of human sexuality.

Confirmation of this fact has come from all the major health and mental health organizations—including the American Psychiatric and Psychological Associations, the American Academy of Pediatrics, and the National Association of Social Workers, among many others—which have all come to recognize that homosexuality is not deviant, not a symptom or category of illness, but simply *normal*.

You may have heard of people who claim to have changed their orientation. They appear to be confusing *behavior, identity,* and *orientation*. They may have been able to stop acting on their attraction, and they may have publicly identified themselves as heterosexual, but nothing has been found to change people's internal *orientation*.

A person's sexual orientation isn't chosen but discovered.

Why do people need to "come out"? Isn't sexuality a private matter?

Just for a moment, let's consider the ways that heterosexual people "come out" about their orientation without feeling that they're sharing private information. For example, they talk about their spouse or special friend, they hold hands and embrace in public, or they carry photos into their workplace. These activities *express* sexuality and yet are taken for granted as normal and acceptable.

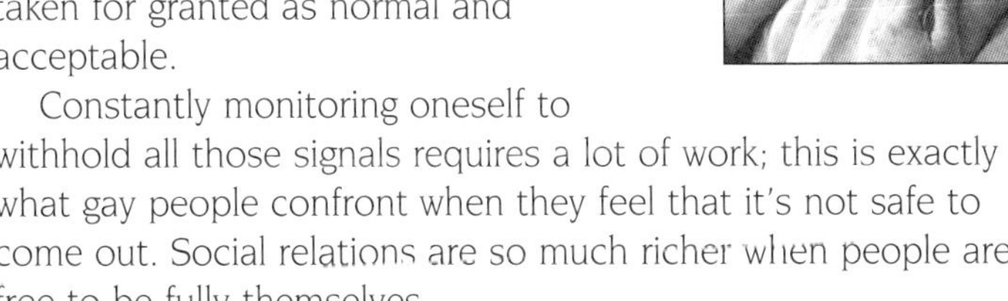

Constantly monitoring oneself to withhold all those signals requires a lot of work; this is exactly what gay people confront when they feel that it's not safe to come out. Social relations are so much richer when people are free to be fully themselves.

Are bisexual people going through a stage?

Our society tries to simplify attraction—something that's extremely complex—into two polar opposites: Either you're heterosexual or you're gay/lesbian. But not everyone's experience fits that oversimplification. For bisexuals, the other person's biological sex may not play as large a role in their attractions as other personal characteristics.

It does happen sometimes that gay/lesbian people will begin their coming-out by thinking and saying that they're bisexual, which may seem safer to them at first. But it also often happens that many people who are bisexual never mention it. That, coupled with society's insistence on only two possible sexual orientations, supports the impression that bisexuality is rare. It's not. Actually, it's quite common.

Photos © Limor Inbar/Indelible Images (top) and © The Point Foundation (bottom)

Social relations are so much richer when people are free to be fully themselves.

Photo © Arnold Gold/*New Haven Register*/The Image Works

What do same-sex couples do together?

Just like other-sex couples, same-sex couples pursue whatever interests they have in common—singing, playing ball, gardening, worshipping, raising families, and so on. They have the same potential for positive and negative relating—caring, hurting, nurturing, fighting, having fun, abusing, competing, or cooperating. They also have available the same means for making love—holding hands, intimate eye contact, and touching with every part of the body.

Why do gay and lesbian people want to marry?

Think about why heterosexual couples want to marry. They love each other, and they want to commit their lives to each other. Often they feel that it's important to publicly declare their union—to make a commitment in the context of their religious community or among family and friends.

And, of course, when people marry, they gain hundreds of legal rights and benefits, both public and private, including the right to visit their spouse in the hospital, a safety net for their children, family leave, and medical insurance, as well as retirement and inheritance benefits.

What's it like to grow up gay/lesbian/bisexual?

Again, there's no simple answer because everyone is unique and we have so many different racial, ethnic, family, cultural, and religious backgrounds.

But to get a glimpse of what it's like, call to mind a three-year-old child in your life—perhaps your own child or grandchild, a niece, a neighbor, or a child in your congregation. Assume for a moment that this child will discover that he or she is gay, lesbian, or bisexual. Remember also that people's self-image is often a mirror of what they've heard or absorbed from the important people around them.

Now recall all the messages about homosexuality that you heard when *you* were growing up—words spoken by your parents, extended family, and religious leaders—and imagine that this child is hearing all those same words. What might this child's self-image be?

The problem comes not from being gay, but from living in a fearful, condemning world.

Now consider this child's experience in the community. He or she may be taunted and bullied at school or in the neighborhood, rejected by family and friends (possibly even kicked out of the house), physically abused, discriminated against, isolated, and more.

Such youth often decide that it's easier to be invisible, to distance themselves from their families and peers. They may monitor everything they say or do so as not to give themselves away. For too many of them, there's nowhere to talk openly.

Make no mistake. These problems don't come from being gay, lesbian, or bisexual; they come from living in a fearful, condemning world.

As circumstances change in some localities, youth can find affirmation through support groups, school-based gay/straight alliances, and community services. And a few really lucky ones have parents and congregations that mean it when they say, "You're a child of God, and we love you for yourself."

Scripture

not condemnation, but love

For several centuries, the official church has promoted the view that the Bible condemns homosexuality. Those who oppose it hold up a half a dozen passages to support their beliefs, in much the same way that people used to cite the Bible to justify slavery.

Before talking about what the Bible says and doesn't say about homosexuality, it's important to note that people today use the Bible in widely different ways.

Step back and consider for a moment how you use it. What authority does the Bible have in your life? Do you look only to the words themselves for guidance, or do you also consider

- Historical information about the social and cultural context?
- Current knowledge and understanding?
- Traditions of your denomination or ethnic/cultural group?
- Your own life experiences and those of others?

If you're reading this booklet with a study/prayer group, think about how your mutual reading of the Bible helps you to be faithful to God and to be Christ's church in the world.

What does it mean to be a community of faith that roots itself in the Bible and especially in Jesus' teaching?

One thing is clear: The Bible does contain some problematic messages. For example, most of us would reject Lot's offering his young daughters for gang rape (Gen. 19:8), Leviticus' mandate to impose the death penalty for cursing (Lev. 24:14), and Paul's view that a woman's head should be shaved if she prays without a veil (I Cor. 11:5–16).

By the same token, we must not allow half a dozen passages to override Jesus' central message of love and reconciliation.

In the photo above, Rev. Dr. Janie Spahr, denied ordination because she is a lesbian, comforts a supporter.

What does the Bible really say about homosexuality?

First, *nowhere* does the Bible condemn loving, faithful relationships of any kind. Indeed, there are stories throughout the Bible celebrating emotionally deep, caring, intimate, same-sex relationships—for example, between Ruth and Naomi, David and Jonathan, and Jesus and his disciples.

In fact, in Biblical times, the Israelites didn't think about sexuality in terms of *sexual orientation, identity,* or *behavior*; those concepts have been developed and understood only within the past hundred years.

In Christ's church,

everyone is welcome—everyone.

No one is excluded.

Although analyzing the particular passages that are said to condemn homosexuality is beyond the scope of this booklet, scholars have concluded that the sins being discussed were *other* behaviors and attitudes.

Instead of homosexuality, the sin was inhospitality toward foreigners or strangers, violence, idolatry, rape, prostitution, and sexual abuse and exploitation.

What did Jesus say?

We can't know what Jesus thought or said about homosexuality because there's no report of it in the Bible.

What Jesus is described as doing, time and again, is overturning religious and social traditions whose purpose was to condemn people.

He got very upset, for example, about traditions that required people to make costly sacrifices to prove that they were truly faithful. He could see that the standards were so high that most of us could never meet them.

Even more, Jesus refused to accept traditions that excluded whole groups of people—such as the Gentiles and the Samaritans.

He called into question the catalogue of sins for which people could be stoned to death.

Time and again, He negated traditions that defined standards for condemning people. Instead, He lived a life of love and mercy, responding to those in need.

How ironic and tragic that Christians today are using a few passages in the Bible to justify excluding, condemning, and discriminating against people—the very thing that Jesus railed against.

What was Jesus telling us? Simply that God doesn't divide us into "we" and "they," that God's grace has been made available to *all* of us. Jesus' amazing message then and now is that God loves and accepts each of us. We don't have to qualify based on who we are or what we do or don't do. Love and acceptance are gifts of God.

If we love one another,
God's love
is made complete in us.

In our diverse world, we'll never reach complete consensus on theological issues. What we do know, however, is that reconciliation and grace have come to all of us—without exception—as a gift through Jesus Christ.

Given that, we cannot justify excluding a whole group of people, as the Church has done with those who are gay, lesbian, or bisexual. In Christ's church, everyone is welcome.

N*o one has ever seen God; but if we love one another, God lives in us and God's love is made complete in us.*

—1 *John* 4:12

PEOPLE

within the Church

LESBIAN, GAY, AND BISEXUAL PEOPLE

- Live in Everytown, USA
- Are black, white, Hispanic, American Indian, and Asian
- Laugh, cry, eat, sleep, work, and worry like everyone else
- Serve in parishes and church agencies, teach Sunday school, sing in the choir, serve as ministers and even bishops
- Make music, dig ditches, perform heart surgery, pick up trash, sell antiques, teach school, drive taxis, grow food, and serve in the government and the military
- Make a lifetime commitment to another person
- Conceive and raise children
- Are poor, middle class, and affluent
- Are sons and daughters, brothers and sisters, cousins, nieces and nephews, and grandchildren
- Are mothers and fathers, aunts and uncles, and grandparents

EXPERIENCES OF REAL PEOPLE: HOW WOULD YOU FEEL IF

...Your life partner of 40 years was in intensive care and you weren't allowed to visit because you're not considered family?

...You knew that other kids in your class invited each other over, but nobody ever accepted your invitation? They never say why, but you think it's because their parents are wary of a family with two dads.

...Your partner had just died and his parents, ignoring the fact that you'd been together for 12 years, were coming to dismantle and sell the house you'd shared?

...You got a phone call telling you that three people were beaten by a gang screaming anti-gay/lesbian epithets? One of the victims, your sister, is in critical condition.

...You were a single, gay man in seminary, and your married classmates were all looking forward to moving into a parsonage after ordination? You, however, worry about what will happen when you find someone you want to settle down with.

...You were 16 and all the other girls were talking about boys, but you were attracted to girls? Should you share your feelings? Should you make up stories to protect your secret?

Gay/lesbian/bisexual people are sons and daughters, fathers and mothers, grandparents...

...After months of trying to work things out, you and your partner of seven years decided to separate? The next Sunday, the minister announces a new support group for people going through a divorce. Should you join the group and share your pain?

...The new senior pastor saw your name in a gay-friendly church publication and convinced the church council to demand your immediate resignation? You've been the Director of Christian Education and Youth Ministry for 17 years and have been loved by a generation of children and their families.

...You told your father how much you and your partner were looking forward to coming to Aunt Mary's for Thanksgiving, and he replied that you were welcome, but your partner wasn't?

...You couldn't eat lunch in peace in your high school cafeteria, because the other students were calling you "faggot" and "girlie" and throwing food at you, while the teachers stood by and did nothing?

...Your partner was going to work in a war zone for six weeks? Would it be safe to embrace and kiss at the airport, as you see other couples doing?

...You and your partner both wanted to attend the PTA open house at your child's school, but doing so would, in effect, announce to the school that your child has two moms?

More experiences of real people

How much do you know about

- Hitler's slaughter of thousands of gay people during the Holocaust?
- Official inattention to beatings, even murders, of people who are or are believed to be lesbian or gay?
- The ability of employers in most states to fire workers simply because they're gay or lesbian?
- The military's policy of discharging personnel who acknowledge that they're gay or lesbian?

Photo © Rachel Epstein/The Image Works

Even the perception that a person is gay/lesbian is often enough to trigger hostility.

- Citizens' having no right to petition for their same-sex partners to immigrate?
- Gay and lesbian people being denied protections or benefits, such as access to a hospital room, health insurance, parenting privileges, or Social Security survivor benefits?
- Hostile name-calling and bullying in schools on a daily basis?

Actual experiences of reconciliation in the church

"When I was 13, I already knew that I was different from the other boys, but I didn't fully understand it yet. Then one day my Sunday School teacher said something—I don't even know the words she used—that let me know that whoever I figured out I was, I was okay with her and with God. Her brief remarks supported me through a lot of trouble over the next several years."

"Finally I feel included; our new pastor never fails to lift up the concerns of lesbian, gay, and bi people in sermons and prayers."

Photo © Mark Richards/Photo Edit

"My partner and I were asked to be godparents for our friends' newborn. Participating in her baptism was one of the most spiritually moving moments of our relationship."

"When I learned that my friend—the one who helped me survive my separation and divorce— was gay, I found that keeping our friendship was more important to me than keeping my mind closed about homosexuality."

"I was in college when my mother told us that she was moving in with Liz. She made it clear that they were more than friends, and I really struggled with that at first. But I can remember how hard it was for her to be married to my father, and I see how much happier she is. We're closer than ever."

"My Sunday School teacher let me know that I was okay with her and with God."

"At my children's school, the worst names the kids can think of calling each other are 'fag' and 'dyke.' At least at church they're getting a positive message that helps them feel good about our family. That means so much to me."

"When my partner was dying, members of the congregation brought food and sent such loving notes. I don't know what I would have done without them."

"We were both raised in the church, and the thought of having our wedding anywhere else never occurred to us. We're so grateful to be part of a welcoming congregation. Families opened their homes to our relatives, put on the reception for us, and even hosted a bridal shower."

"After my son came out to me, I was tormented by the thought of what he'd been listening to me say about gays all those years, parroting the words of our church. We immediately found a church where our whole family was welcome."

Three elected officials from Florida.

An invitation

join us on our journey

In this booklet, we've tried to give an overview of some very complex issues facing us personally and as a church. If you're just beginning to explore these issues, you'll need two things: an open heart and more educational resources.

The most important and helpful resources are openly lesbian, gay, and bisexual people, as well as their parents and families. If you don't know who those people are—or if you aren't in a position to speak openly yourself—you could seek out a group that provides speakers who have volunteered to share their own personal experiences. On the next pages are some suggestions to get you started.

In a spirit of love and justice

We as individuals and religious communities have some soul searching to do. Dumbarton Church continues to ask these questions, and we urge you to ask them as well:

- As part of an institutional church and a society that regularly condemn homosexuality, what does Jesus ask of us?
- Can we truly acknowledge human sexuality as a "good gift of God"?
- Can we love our neighbors—whatever their or our sexual orientation—as ourselves?
- Can we support those among us who strive to establish loving, enriching, committed relationships of whatever sexual orientation?
- Can we reach out with love to people who are hurting, whatever their sexual orientation might be?
- Will we help build a safe, just, and compassionate society for all of God's children?

That's the challenge. God be with you on your journey!

For more information

Films/videos

- *All God's Children: Exploring Homophobia in the African American Community* (1996); *I Exist: Voices from the Lesbian and Gay Middle Eastern Community* (2004), www.unlearninghomophobia.com/agc.html
- *It's Elementary: Talking about Gay Issues in School* (1997); *That's a Family: A Film for Kids about Family Diversity* (2000); *Let's Get Real: Kids Speak up about Bullying* (2003), Debra Chasnoff and Helen Cohen, Women's Educational Media, www.womedia.org
- *Trembling Before G-d*, Sandi Simcha Dubowski (2001), www.tremblingbeforeg-d.com

Print resources

- *Claiming the Promise: An Ecumenical Welcoming Bible Study Resource on Homosexuality*, Mary Jo Osterman, Reconciling Ministries Network, 2004
- *Coming Out While Staying In: Struggles and Celebrations of Lesbians, Gays, and Bisexuals in the Church*, Leanne Tigert, United Church Press, 1996
- *Families Like Mine*, Abigail Garner, HarperCollins Publishers, 2004
- *What If Someone I Know Is Gay? Answers to Questions about Gay and Lesbian People* (for grades 7–10), Eric Marcus, Price Stern Sloan, 2000
- *What Is Marriage For? The Strange Social History of Our Most Intimate Institution*, E. J. Graff, Beacon Press, 1999
- *What the Bible Really Says about Homosexuality*, Daniel A. Helminiak, Ph.D., Millenium Edition, New Mexico, Alamo Square Press, 2000

Organizations

- COLAGE, *Children of Lesbians and Gays Everywhere*, 415–861–5437, www.colage.org
- *Family Pride Coalition*, 202–331–5015, www.familypride.org
- GLSEN, *the Gay, Lesbian and Straight Education Network*, 212–727–0135, www.glsen.org
- NYAC, *National Youth Advocacy Coalition*, 202-319-7596, www.nyacyouth.org.
- PFLAG, *Parents, Families, and Friends of Lesbians and Gays*, 202–467–8180, www.pflag.org
- *Sex, Etc.*, 732–445–7929, www.sxetc.org (by teens for teens)

Supportive Religious Groups

Affirm United (United Church of Canada)
www.affirmunited.ca

Affirmation: Gay and Lesbian Mormons
323–255–7251, www.affirmation.org

Al-Fatiha, LGBT Muslims and Friends
202–319–0898, www.al-fatiha.org

Association of Welcoming & Affirming Baptists
919–560–7069, www.wabaptists.org

Brethren/Mennonite Council for Lesbian and Gay Concerns
612–343–2060, www.webcom.com/bmc

Dignity USA (Catholic)
800–877–8797, www.dignityusa.org

Frum Gay Jews Everywhere
www.members.tripod.com/~djs28

Gay, Lesbian and Affirming Disciples Alliance
www.gladalliance.org

Lutherans Concerned/North America
www.lcna.org

More Light Presbyterians
www.mlp.org

Reconciling Ministries Network (United Methodist)
773–736–5526, www.rmnetwork.org

Shower of Stoles Project
612-377-8792, www.showerofstoles.org

Soulforce
918–452–3184, www.soulforce.org

Unitarian Universalist Association
617–742–2100, www.uua.org/oblgtc

United Church of Christ Coalition for LGBT *Concerns*
800–653–0799, www.ucccoalition.org

Universal Fellowship of Metropolitan Community Churches
310–360–8640, www.mccchurch.org

World Congress of Gay, Lesbian, Bisexual and Transgender Jews: Keshet Ga'avah
202–452–7424

About the Author

Ann Thompson Cook has been educating people about sexuality, reproductive health, and gender for 25 years. She has written extensively, and her publications include *Made in God's Image* and PFLAG's *Respect All Youth* series. She and her husband of 35 years have two adult sons.

Acknowledgments

Many thanks to David Cook and the countless other friends and colleagues who contributed to this booklet and also to the people who agreed to have their photos published. In particular, Dumbarton's pastor, Rev. Dr. Mary Kraus, along with Rev. Dr. William D. (Chip) Aldridge, Rev. Nancy Webb, Laurie Coburn, Cheryl Conway, Thew Elliott, William J. Matson, Cindy Pomeroy, Chett Pritchett, Jay Pryor, Monika Ruppert, Sally Sparks, Jenn Whatley, and many others generously supported the planning and writing.

And special thanks to the following expert advisers:

Mark Bowman, M.Div., Co-Founder
Reconciling Ministries Network

Mary E. Hunt, Ph.D., Co-Director
Women's Alliance for Theology, Ethics, and Ritual

Lis Maurer, Coordinator
Center for LGBT Education, Outreach, & Services, Ithaca College

Jerald Newberry, Executive Director
National Education Association Health Information Network

Melany Burrill
Joan Garrity
Elizabeth Schroeder, MSW
Pamela M. Wilson, MSW
Wayne Pawlowski, ACSW, LICSW
Sexuality Educators, Professional Trainers/Consultants

In grateful memory:
Doug Hinckle, Rev. Penny Penrose and Mary Lee Tatum, M.Ed.

The development of this booklet was supported in part by a generous grant from the E. Rhodes and Leona B. Carpenter Foundation.

Designed by Barbara L. Salthouse.
Design of the first edition by The Page Group, Inc.